The Surname Cruise

Wendy Bosberry-Scott
& Susan Morris

ISBN: 1537015524
ISBN-13: 978-1537015521

The question of surnames, their origins, distribution and history, lies at the heart of genealogy as well as being fascinating in its own right.

In the 1980s and 1990s, long before many genealogical sources were even indexed, let alone online, our Surname Report service provided expert assessments of the origins, history and distribution of selected British surnames, using the sources available at the time.

Now, with so many more sources available, we believe that these reports retain their value as studies of individual surnames, and so we are gradually making the Debrett Surname Archive available online and in print for the first time. Some modern indexes have been consulted to refresh and update the reports.

Debrett Ancestry Research Ltd, PO Box 379,
Winchester SO23 9YQ
Tel: 01962 841904
Email: info@debrettancestry.co.uk
Website: www.debrettancestry.co.uk

CONTENTS

Overview

The use of surnames in England began in the Norman period, when surnames were not necessarily hereditary but usually a form of description. Some described the individual's trade or profession; others were nicknames; some gave the father's Christian name; others gave the individual's place of residence or origin.

Different surnames might be used in different documents, or more than one surname given in one document. Early descriptions were fairly elaborate and by the thirteenth and fourteenth centuries these were simpler, but still variable, and indeed the instability of surnames continued until well into the seventeenth century.

Although some Normans would already have had hereditary surnames on their arrival in Britain, the passing on of a surname from generation to generation only became customary in Britain gradually during the course of the thirteenth and fourteenth centuries. At the end of this period most of the population apparently had surnames.

Variations in the spelling of a family's surname continue to be found until the present century. Before this, as most people could not read or write, the parish clerk or other official would write down the name as they heard it.

There are four main groups of surnames:

A – Local names, which describe a person by his place of residence or origin.

B – Occupational names, which describe a person by his trade or profession.

C – Surnames of relationship, which refer to the Christian name of the father or other important relative.

D – Nicknames or sobriquets, coined to describe a person in terms of his appearance or character.

The name Cruise (which in this report is treated together with its variants Crew(e)s, Cruse, Cruwys, Cruyce, Cruys, Cruze and Crwys) falls into Categories A and D.

Origins and Early Examples

Two possible sources have been identified for the name Cruise.

(i)   from the Old English *Cr(o)use(e)*, a nickname meaning bold or fierce.

(ii)   P H Reaney's authoritative *Dictionary of English Surnames* suggests that one medieval instance of the name may refer to the place name Cruys-Straete in Normandy.

The surname appears as Cruwys in Devon as early as 1166 (see below). The earliest individual example cited in standard reference works is Nicholas Le Cruise of Bedfordshire, 1213 (Curia Regis Rolls, cited by Reaney, *op cit*). A Nicholas Le Cruse also appears in the Hundred Rolls for Bedfordshire in 1279.

Other early examples of the surname are as follows:

1214	Richard de Crues, Curia Regis Rolls, Devon
pre 1242	Alexander de Crues, Fees, owner of Cruyws Morchard, Devon
1279	Robert Creuse, Bedfordshire Hundred Rolls

Reaney suggests that Richard de Crues might have had origins in Cruys-Straete, Normandy, while Nicholas Le Cruse might have been an original 'fierce' character (or perhaps the opposite - nicknames could be ironic) to whom the name was applied.

Reaney's suggestion with regard to Cruys-Straete is repeated by Eilert Ekwall (*Oxford Dictionary of Place-Names*) in his discussion of the Devon place-name Cruwys Morchard, which reflects the name of its landowning family and appears in 1281 as *Morcestr' Crues*. (Morchard means 'great wood'.)

We thus see here two separate strands, one in Devon possibly deriving from a Norman place name and one in Bedfordshire deriving from a nickname, but the medieval evidence is too sparse to provide a clear pattern.

Distribution

The existing volumes of the *English Surname Series* (which is very incomplete) provide scholarly and detailed modern studies of surnames. In the volume for Devon (David Postles, 1995) the Cruwys family is mentioned as one of several landowning families of knightly status who appear in a Pipe Roll of 1166 and whose names survive locally as hereditary surnames.

David Postles also cites the Reverend W M Birch's nineteenth-century article on the parish registers of Ashburton and Buckland in the Moor:

> In 1896, the Rev W M Birch remarked upon the continuity of surnames in Ashburton from 1603, when the registers are extant, through to his own time, including ... Cruse ...

Postles distinguishes between these names and the surname de la Cruce which he groups with Cross. This distinction is also made by Richard McKinley in his earlier Oxfordshire volume (1977). In our survey we have noted examples of the surname Cruyce (etc) but these may have a separate derivation from Cruise/Crewes etc: as with all surnames, before printing and literacy was widespread, variation of spelling was the norm and it is likely that names with different derivations have interchanged and mingled.

In 1890 H B Guppy published his *Homes of Family Names in Great Britain*, still the only published work on surname distribution in Britain as a whole. His work was based on printed genealogies and a survey of county directories for the 1880s, in which he looked especially at the names of farmers, reasoning that they were among the most stable groups in society. He noted that the name Cruse or Cruwys was sometimes modernised as Crews, and is the name of a very ancient and distinguished Devon family of Netherex. However, he found the name to be scarce in Devon at the time of his publication.

Many of the sources available for charting surname distribution through the centuries are necessarily confined to the wealthier sectors of the population: in general, nobody wanted to know the names of the poor but the names of those with money or land were naturally of interest to the authorities. However, one source that covers the whole of the social spectrum is provided by English parish registers, the earliest of which began in 1538 following a mandate that all parish priests should keep a weekly record of all baptisms, marriages and burials that took place in their parish. A survey of a cross section of parish registers for the years 1601 and 1602 was carried out in 1910 by F K and S Hitching; incidences of a particular surname are noted by parish and county, although with no indication of numbers of references.

They noted the appearance of Crewe, but there were no references to Cruise or its variants.

Scottish records of births, baptisms, marriages and deaths are now indexed online for the period 1553 to 1953. Using this index we found very few entries for the name:

Old Parish Registers:
Births & Christenings 1553-1854

Crewes	1
Crews	2
Cruise	1

Statutory Registration: Births 1855-1904

Crewes	1
Crews	18
Cruise	6
Cruse	42
Cruys	1

Old Parish Registers: Banns & Marriages 1553-1854

Crewes	1
Crews	2
Cruise	2
Cruse	2

Statutory Registration: Banns & Marriages 1855-1929

Crews	16
Cruise	4
Cruse	36
Cruwys	1
Cruys	1
Cruze	1

Statutory Registration: Deaths 1855-1954

Crewes	2
Crews	38
Cruise	23
Cruse	52
Cruze	1

The very low numbers for the surname Cruise and its variants in Scottish records indicate its rarity in the north of the United Kingdom.

Edward McLysaght's *Surnames of Ireland* tells us that Cruise (in Gaelic *de Cruis*) is found consistently as 'de Cruys' and not 'le Cruys' in medieval Irish sources, indicating a place name origin. In Ireland the Cruise family is:

> One of the oldest of the Hiberno-Norman families, mainly identified with Cos. Meath and Dublin.

A useful guide to the distribution of surnames for the sixteenth, seventeenth and eighteenth centuries in England is provided by the indexes to wills proved, and administrations granted, at the Prerogative Court of (the Archbishop of) Canterbury, in London, which had superior jurisdiction over local ecclesiastical courts where wills were proved until 1858. The PCC thus provides a national index, although it is not a completely representative one, as testators whose wills were proved in the PCC were mostly among the wealthier members of society, and a disproportionate number of them were from London or Middlesex. The PCC was the usual court used for testators who died abroad. We found the following entries for Cruise (etc):

Sixteenth Century
1502   William Cruise, haberdasher of London
1577   John Cruse, of Morchard Cruwys, Devon
1586   Anne Cruse, widow of Moretonhampstead, Devon
1592   John Cruse, yeoman of Wootton Bassett, Wiltshire

Very few entries were found for the sixteenth century. It was interesting to see a testator from Morchard Cruwys using the form Cruse.

Seventeenth Century

1615 Gilbert Crewes of Gerrans, Cornwall

1625 Robert Cruse, Grocer, St Pancras London

1629 Thomas Cruse or Croues, husbandman of North Horly, Hampshire

1642 Thomas Cruse, gentleman of Ashburton, Devon

1645 William Cruse, mercer of Dulverton, Somerset

1645 William Crewes, gentleman of London

1645 Jefferie Crewes, gentleman of His Majesty's Fyfe in Ordinary of Lambeth, Surrey

1646 Joane Cruse, widow of Dulverton, Somerset

1647 Nicholas Cruse of Morebath, Devon

1648 Alexander Cruse

1648 Susann Cruse, wife of Winkleigh, Devon

1651 George Cruse, gentleman of Ashton, Devon

1652 William Cruse, yeoman of Ashwater, Devon

1655 Mary Cruse, wife of Winkleigh, Devon

1656 Robert Crewes, vintner of London

1666 Robert Cruys, gentleman of Richmond, Surrey

1667 Thomas Cruse, gentleman of Witheridge

1676 Robert Cruys, master of arts at the University of Oxford

1688 John Cruys, bachelor of Aldersgate Street, City of London

1689 Vincenty Cruse, bachelor

1692 Richard Cruse, mariner of Devon

The majority of the entries found for the seventeenth century were from Devon and all used the form Cruse. We have a Crewes in the neighbouring county of Cornwall and the rarer variant, Cruys, was found in Oxford, London and Surrey.

Eighteenth Century

1700 Charles Cruse, gentleman of Wootton Bassett, Wiltshire

1702   Robert Crews, mariner of St Paul Shadwell,
       Middlesex

1707   Richard Cruise, mariner of Stepney, Middlesex

1708   Gabriel Cruse, grazier of Wootton Bassett,
       Wiltshire

1709   John Crewes, Cruse or Crews, mariner of St
       Botolph without Aldgate, London

1709   Edward Cruse, distiller of St George the
       Martyr, Southwark, Surrey

1711   Emm Cruse, widow of St George, Southwark,
       Surrey

1712   John Cruwys of Cruwys Morchard, Devon

1714   Francis Cruys, gentleman of St Martin in the
       Fields, Middlesex

1718   Gaynor Cruise, widow of St Nicholas in
       Worcester, Worcestershire

1718   Oliver Crewes, buttonmaker of Sherborne,
       Dorset

1725   William Cruce or Cruse of St George,
       Southwark, Surrey

1729   John Crews or Crewes, butcher of Long
       Crendon, Buckinghamshire

1729   Adrian Van de Cruys of Amsterdam

1732   Robert Crews, victualler of New Thame,
       Oxfordshire

1736   Matthew or Matthews Crewes or Crews, tallow
       chandler of Thame, Oxfordshire

1739   Edward Crews of St Columb Major, Cornwall,
       sentence

1740   Stephen de la Cruze of St Giles in the Fields,
       Middlesex

1742   Christiaan Cruys of Amsterdam, Holland

1746   Peter Cruise or Krus otherwise Cruse, mariner
       belonging to His Majesty's Ship *Chichester*, of
       Stockholm

1749   Thomas Crews, tallow chandler of Thame,
       Oxfordshire

1751   Elizabeth Cruwys, spinster of Exeter, Devon

1756 Susanna Cruwys, widow of St Clement Danes, Middlesex

1757 Dorothy Cruwys, of St Martin Westminster, Middlesex

1759 Lady Maria Mechthildis, otherwise Mechtildes de Coninck, or Vanden Cruyce, wife of Antwerp

1759 The Honorable Paschasins John Anccustyn Vanden Cruyce, Lord of Aertzelaer Cleydael, Ancient Sheriff and Treasurer General of the City of Antwerp of Antwerp

1760 Henry Cruwys Esq., of Hillersdon, Devon

1760 John Cruse, mariner now belonging to the East India Company now outward bound in the *Bombay Castle*, Pts

1761 Abraham Cruse, mariner belonging to His Majesties Ship *Bristol*, Pts

1763 Nicholas Crews, seaman belonging to his Majesty's Ship *America*, Devon

1764 William Cruse, of St Margaret's Westminster, Middlesex

1765 Elizabeth Cruze, widow of St John Westminster, Middlesex

1765 Jane Cruwys, widow of Hillersden, Devon

1769 Susannah de la Cruze, Middlesex

1770 Thomas Augustus Cruwys, of New Inn, Middlesex

1771 Darvill (Darvil) Crews, butcher of Long Crendon, Buckinghamshire

1780 Henry Crews (aka Cruse), St James, Middlesex

1781 John Crews, gentleman of Bicester, Oxfordshire

1781 Gabriel Cruse, upholder of Devizes, Wiltshire

1782 Mary Cruse, widow of Speen, Berkshire

1782 Martha Crews, widow of Bicester, Market End, Oxfordshire

1783 Elizabeth Cruse, widow of Devizes, Wiltshire

1786 John Cruse, baker of St Gregory, London

1786	Albert Lewis Joseph Van Den Cruyce, Lord of the manor of Wastinne, bachelor of Brussels, Brabant
1787	John Cruwys, labourer of Barking, Essex
1790	Helena Maria Francoise Vanden Cruyce, widow of Antwerp
1791	John Cruwys, Reverend, Devon
1792	Ann Crews, widow of New Thame, Oxfordshire
1794	Sarah Crews, spinster of New Thame, Oxfordshire
1794	Bridget Cruwys, spinster of St Martin in the Fields, Middlesex
1794	William Cruise, carpenter of His Majesty's Ship *Cyclops*
1797	George Cruse, mariner of Townstall, Devon

The testators named Van Den Cruyce from Belgium and Holland have been included in this listing for the sake of interest but these are unlikely to be related to the English surname Cruise (etc). It will be seen that Devon still features strongly in the list, especially considering its distance from London where the court was held. There are a few testators from Wiltshire and Oxfordshire, and one each from Buckinghamshire, Worcestershire, Dorset and Cornwall. The majority of entries relate to London and its environs, which reflects a general trend for the PCC at this period.

Nineteenth Century

1800	Anne Charlotte Cruse, wife of Sheering, Essex
1803	Charles Cruse, gentleman of Wootton Bassett, Wiltshire
1803	John Cruise, seaman belonging to His Majesty's Ship *Leviathan*
1804	Mary Russell formerly Mary Crews, widow of St Giles Cripplegate, Middlesex

1804 Anne Marie Isabelle Vanden Cruyce, spinster of Brussels

1805 Reverend Henry Shortrudge Cruwys, clerk, Doctor in Divinity of Cruwys Morchard, Devon

1809 Loveday Glynn Crews, widow of Bodmin, Cornwall

1810 Richard Cruse other Crues of Carhampton, Somerset

1810 Arnoldus Paschalis otherwise Paschasius, otherwise Paschal Van Den Cruyce, otherwise Venden Cruyce, bachelor of Antwep, Austrian Netherlands

1811 Edward Cruse of Doctor's Commons, Middlesex

1811 Richard Hall commonly called or known by the name of Charles Cruise, marine in His Majesty's Service of St George the Martyr, Surrey

1812 Jane Cruse, spinster of Wootton Bassett, Wiltshire

1818 Jonathan Freak formerly styled Jonathan Cruse of Sheering, Essex

1818 William Cruse, gentleman of St George's Hanover Square, Middlesex

1821 Nicholas Crews, gentleman of St Mewan, Cornwall

1824 William Cruise of Albany Piccadilly, Middlesex

1828 John Crews shipmaster of Greenock, Renfrewshire

1830 Henry Cruse, depositor in the Provident Institution for Savings, bachelor of St Marylebone, Middlesex

1836 Mary Cruse, widow of Dorchester, Oxfordshire

1837 Mary Cruse, spinster of Towcester, Northamptonshire

1838 Archelaus Cruse, news vendor of St Botolph Aldersgate, City of London

1843 Samuel Crews, gentleman of Horsham, Sussex

1847	Louisa Waterhouse heretofore Cruse, wife of 10 Clark Street, Jubilee Place, Commercial Road, Middlesex
1848	Henry Cruse, gentleman of 38 Beaumont Square, Mile End Road, Middlesex
1855	Samuel Crews, yeoman of Kingswood, Surrey
1856	Margaret Cruse, widow of 2 Cambridge Street, Edgware Road, Middlesex
1856	Ellen Cruise, spinster of City of Dublin
1857	Catherine Crews, widow of St Giles in the Fields, Middlesex

Again, the majority of entries here relate to the south-east of England. We find two testators from Cornwall in the nineteenth century and one each from Northamptonshire, Scotland and Ireland. The single Devon entry in this period is for a Cruwys of Cruwys Morchard.

Overall, the PCC indexes support David Postles' observations with regard to the continuity of the name Cruwys (and variants) in Devon right through from medieval times, although the name had also spread widely by the nineteenth century. No references were found from Bedfordshire, where it appeared to have been hereditary in the thirteenth century, and the sprinkling found in the bordering county of Buckinghamshire does not appear until the eighteenth century.

The online index to Scottish testaments (*ScotlandsPeople*) shows just two entries for the name, again indicating its rarity there:

Scottish Wills & Testaments 1513-1901
Name   Numbers of Testators
Crewes   2

For the nineteenth century, H B Guppy's survey has been mentioned above. Another important Victorian source is the *Return of Owners of Land* of 1873, sometimes known as the Modern Domesday Book. This source lists, county by county, every owner of an acre of land or more, with their residence (not necessarily the address of their property) and the acreage of their holding.

Return of Owners of Land (1873)

Cornwall   1   Crews
    (Richard Crews of Grampound, 2 acres)
Surrey   1   Creuze
Worcestershire   1   Crewse

There were no longer any Cruwys (etc) landowners in Devon. There were also many entries for Crew and Crewe, mainly for Lord Crewe of Calke Abbey who owned vast tracts of lands in several counties, mainly in Stafford, Leicestershire, Durham and Derbyshire.

Decennial census returns were instituted in England, Scotland and Wales in 1801. Personal returns survive from 1841 onwards. The latest census currently available is that of 1911 and all have been indexed by surname.

In the United States, the census was instituted in 1790, but prior to 1850 only the head of the household was named. From 1850 onwards, each member of the household was named. The 1890 census returns were destroyed by fire.

We used the census surname indexes to give a broader picture of the distribution of the name Cruise (and variants). We have included the form Cruze although in the US this is more likely to derive from the Hispanic form Cruz which is associated with the distinct group Cross/Delacroix etc.

1790 - United States (heads of household)
Crews – 9; Cruise – 6; Cruse – 16

1800 - United States (heads of household)
Crews – 10; Cruise – 5; Cruse – 10

1810 - United States (heads of household)
Crews – 47; Cruise – 3; Cruse – 17; Cruze – 1

1820 - United States (heads of household)
Crews – 101; Cruise – 13; Cruse – 20

1830 - United States (heads of household)
Crews – 124; Cruise – 11; Cruse – 41; Cruze – 3

1840 - United States (heads of household)
Crewes – 3; Crews – 207; Cruise – 40; Cruse – 78; Cruze – 2

1850 - United States
Crewes – 9; Crews – 1292; Cruise – 307; Cruse – 877; Cruze - 102

1860 - United States
Crewes – 9; Crews – 1706; Cruise – 456; Cruse – 1085; Cruze – 67

1870 - United States
Crewes – 53; Crews – 2492; Cruise – 513; Cruse – 1703; Cruys – 7; Cruze – 107

1880 - United States
Crewes – 41; Crews – 3902; Cruise – 670;
Cruse – 2110; Cruwys – 1; Cruys – 7; Cruze – 217

1900 - United States
Crewes – 41; Crews – 5684; Cruise – 917;
Cruse – 2781; Cruys – 6; Cruze – 261

1910 - United States (heads of household)
Crewes – 36; Crews – 2115; Cruise – 371;
Cruse – 1079; Cruwys – 1; Cruys – 6; Cruze – 121

1920 - United States
Crewes – 64; Crews – 8235; Cruise – 1402;
Cruse – 3805; Cruwys – 3; Cruyce – 2; Cruys – 6;
Cruze – 580

1930 - United States
Crewes – 77; Crews – 9521; Cruise – 1610;
Cruse – 3916; Cruwys – 8; Cruys – 15; Cruze – 1071

Elsdon C Smith, in his *American Surnames* (1969), includes a list of the most common surnames in the United States, taken from a report drawn up the Social Security Department in 1964 (Distribution of Surnames in the Social Security Account Numbers File). He lists Cruz (which as we have mentioned has a separate origin) as the 353rd most popular name, with 68,590 entries; and Crews as the 1325th name, with 21,333 entries. As mentioned above, there may have been some overlap between these two names.

The census numbers show that the surname Crews was by far the most common form of the surname in the US, with Cruse, the most common variant, some way behind.

In the United Kingdom, the reverse was true, with Cruse being the most common of the variants:

1851
England
    Crewes – 50; Crews – 440; Cruise – 106; Cruse – 484;
    Cruwys – 45; Cruys – 6; Cruze – 7
Isle of Man
    Cruise – 5
Wales
    Crews – 2; Cruise – 1; Cruse – 3

1861
England
    Crewes – 64; Crews – 481; Cruise – 152; Cruse – 589;
    Cruze – 39; Cruwys – 56; Cruys – 4
Scotland
    Crews – 5; Cruise – 1; Cruse – 4
Wales
    Crews – 14; Cruise – 1; Cruse – 3; Cruwys – 7

1871
England
    Crewes – 69; Crews – 555; Cruise – 215; Cruse – 677;
    Cruwys – 61; Cruys – 3; Crwys – 6; Cruze – 22
Scotland
    Cruise – 1; Cruse – 3
Wales
    Crews – 13; Cruse – 2

1881
Channel Islands
    Crews – 2
England
    Crewes – 84; Crews – 519; Cruise – 278; Cruse – 851;
    Cruwys – 75; Cruys – 4; Cruze – 79
Scotland
    Crews – 3; Cruise – 6; Cruse – 3

Wales
  Crews – 2; Cruise – 8; Cruse – 16; Cruwys – 9;
  Cruze – 1

1891
Channel Islands
  Crews – 15; Cruise – 1; Cruze – 1
England
  Crewes – 119; Crews – 558; Cruise – 270; Cruse – 841;
  Cruwys – 46;   Cruys – 4; Cruze – 66
Scotland
  Crews – 9; Cruise – 6; Cruse – 24
Wales
  Crewes – 3; Crews – 32; Cruise – 16; Cruse – 15;
  Cruwys – 14; Cruze –2

1901
Channel Islands
  Crews – 13; Cruse – 2
England
  Crewes – 112; Crews – 655; Cruise – 356; Cruse – 847;
  Cruwys – 59; Cruze – 71
Scotland
  Crewes – 9; Crews – 7; Cruise – 13; Cruse – 40
Wales
  Crews – 29; Cruise – 30; Cruse – 32; Cruze – 3

Famous bearers of the name

The *Oxford Dictionary of National Biography* includes an entry for William Cruise (1751/2–1824) who was an Irish Roman Catholic legal writer from Rathugh in County Westmeath. In modern times the most famous bearer of the name is probably the American actor Tom Cruise (born 1962).

There are a number of Cruse, Cruwys, Creuze, Crewes and Crews coats of arms listed in Burke's *General Armory*.

Printed Genealogies

The following references have been found to printed genealogies of Cruise families and their variants:

Creuze/Cruse

The Genealogist, New Series, '*Some Poitevin Protestants in London*', (H H Sturmer, 1896), xxvii, 114, 35, 40, 60
J L Vivian, *The Visitations of Devon*, 256
Herald and Genealogist, I, 259

Crewes/Crews

Sir J Maclean, *An Historical and Genealogical Memoir of the family of Poyntz*, - published 1886.
Harleian Society, ix, 56
F T Colby (Ed), *Visitations of Devon*, 74
Bibliotheca Topographica Britannica, iv, part vi, 112
J L Vivian (Ed), *The Visitations of Cornwall*, 122
J L Vivian (Ed), *The Visitations of Devon*, 59
Metcalfe, *Visitations of Northamptonshire*, 16

Cruise/Cruis/Cruys/Cruwys

The Genealogist, New Series, xxxiii, 8
M C S Cruwys, *A Cruwys Morchard Notebook 1066-1874*, published 1939
The Genealogist, New Series, xix, 29, 245; xx, 89
Misc. Genealogy and Heraldry, 5th series, ix, 113
Visitations of England and Wales, Notes, vii, 10
Devon and Cornwall, Notes and Queries, xiii, 136
V J Watney, *The Wallop Family and Their Ancestry*, pg. 243, published 1928
Tuckett's Devonshire Pedigrees, 177
Harleian Society, vi, 79

Burke's Landed Gentry, 5, 6, 7, 8
G Oliver and P Jones (Ed), *Westcote's Devonshire*, 516
The Genealogist, New Series, viii, 242
Howard's Visitation of England and Wales, vii, 25

Summary

To conclude, the name Cruise/Crews etc probably originated in some instances as a nickname and in others as a local name, possibly from Normandy. Through the centuries the name has appeared mainly in the south of England, notably in Devon, where there appears to have been a continuity of use of the name Cruse/Cruwys from the twelfth to at least the nineteenth centuries. The name also appears in Ireland from medieval times, apparently deriving from a place name.

The large numbers in the United States using the form Crews may reflect overlap with the Hispanic name Cruz, which has a separate history. Some interchange of the forms Cruise/Crewes and the separate name Crew(e) may also have occurred.

Sources Consulted

P H Reaney, *The Origins of English Surnames* (London: Routledge & Kegan Paul, 1967)

P H Reaney & R M Wilson, *A Dictionary of British Surnames* (Oxford: Oxford University Press, 3rd edition, 1995)

P H Reaney, *Dictionary of British Surnames* (London: Routledge & Kegan Paul, 2nd edition, 1976)

P Hanks & F Hodges, *A Dictionary of Surnames* (Oxford University Press, 1988)

M A Lower, *Patronymica Brittanica* (London, 1860)

C W Bardsley, *Dictionary of English and Welsh Surnames* (1901: reprinted, Baltimore: Genealogical Publishing Co, 1967)

C L'Estrange Ewen, *Guide to the Origin of British Surnames* (London: John Gifford, 1938)

H B Guppy, Homes of Family Names in Great Britain (London, 1890)

Ernest Weekley, *The Romance of Names* (London: John Murray, 2nd edition, 1917)

Ernest Weekley, *Surnames* (London: John Murray, 1917)

George F Black, *The Surnames of Scotland* (New York Public Library, 1946)

Edward McLysaght, *The Surnames of Ireland* (Dublin: Irish University Press, 1977)

T J & Prys Morgan, *Welsh Surnames* (Cardiff: University of Wales Press, 1985)

F K & S Hitching, *References to English Surnames in 1601* (Walton on Thames: Bernau, 1910)

F K & S Hitching, *References to English Surnames in 1602* (Walton on Thames: Bernau, 1911)

Debrett's People of Today (Debrett's Peerage Limited: London, 1996)

The Concise Dictionary of National Biography, Part II, 1901–1950, (Oxford, 1961)

The Oxford Dictionary of National Biography (online, 2004–2014)

Burke's Family Index (London: Burke's Peerage Limited, 1976)

H R Moulton, *Palaeography, Genealogy & Topography* (Sale Catalogue, 1930)

Index to Prerogative Court of Canterbury Wills (The National Archives: online)

G W Marshall, *The Genealogist's Guide* (1903; reprinted, Baltimore: GPC 1973)

J B Whitmore, *A Genealogical Guide* (London, 1953)

Charles Bridge, *An Index to Pedigrees* (London, 1867)

Geoffrey B Barrow, *The Genealogist's Guide* (London: Research Publishing Co, 1977)

Sir Bernard Burke, *The General Armory* (London, 1884)

C R Humphrey-Smith, editor, *Burke's General Armory Volume II*, (Tabard Press, 1973)

The Return of Owners of Land (1873)

Eilert Ekwall, *The Concise Oxford Dictionary of English Place-Names* (Oxford: Clarendon Press, 4th edition, 1960)

E G Withycombe, *The Oxford Dictionary of English Christian Names* (Oxford: Clarendon Press, 2nd edition, 1950)

W J Hardy & W Page, A Calendar to the Feet of Fines for London and Middlesex: Vol 1 Richard I – Richard III (1189–1485) (London, 1892)

Richard McKinley, *The Surnames of Oxfordshire* (English Surnames Series III: Leopard's Head Press, 1977)

Richard McKinley, *The Surnames of Sussex* (English Surnames Series V: Leopard's Head Press, 1988)

Richard McKinley, *The Surnames of Lancashire* (English Surnames Series IV: Leopard's Head Press, 1981)

Richard McKinley, *Norfolk and Suffolk Surnames in the Middle Ages* (English Surnames Series II: Phillimore, 1975)

George Redmonds, *Yorkshire West Riding* (English Surnames Series I: Phillimore, 1973)

Mr Avenell, *The Norman People* (London, 1874)

Debrett's Heraldry (London, 1933)

J P Brooke-Little, revised, *Boutell's Heraldry* (Frederick Warne: London, 1970)

Indexes to 1841–1901 Census Returns of England and Wales (The National Archives/*Ancestry.com*)

Indexes to the 1790-1930 census returns of America (*Ancestry.com*)

Elsdon C Smith, *American Surnames* (GPC, 1969)

ScotlandsPeople: Indexes to Old Parish Registers, Testaments, Statutory Registers

www.ingramcontent.com/pod-product-compliance
Lightning Source LLC
Chambersburg PA
CBHW060443290526
45793CB00002B/559